For Pru

Here's to yours

Marilyn

Sitting Among The Hoppers

Marilyn Longstaff

Marilyn Longstaff

ARROWHEAD
PRESS

First published 2004 by:
Arrowhead Press
70 Clifton Road, Darlington,
Co. Durham, DL1 5DX
Tel: (01325) 260741

Typeset in 11pt Laurentian by
Arrowhead Press

Email: editor@arrowheadpress.co.uk
Website: http://www.arrowheadpress.co.uk

ISBN 1-904852-05-X

Arrowhead Press acknowledges the financial assistance of Arts Council England, North East

Arrowhead Press is a member of Independent Northern Publishers

Printed by Athenaeum Press, Gateshead, Tyne and Wear.

in memory of

my Mum

Acknowledgements

The author is grateful to New Writing North for a Northern Promise Award in 2003 which enabled her to receive mentoring from Andy Croft and S.J.Litherland.

Thanks are due to the editors of the following publications in which some of the poems in this book have been published or accepted for publication:

Magazines: *Coffee House, Envoi, Fire, Interpreter's House, Iota, Other Poetry, Penniless Press, Raindog, Red Herring, Sand, Smiths Knoll, The Rialto.*

Anthologies:

Northern Grit – Vane Women Press
Rewriting The Map – Shore Women/Vane Women
Smelter – Mudfog

Websites:

Franks Casket

Waiting Room was Runner-up in the Ottakars Northallerton Poetry Competition 2003

Cover picture
Summertime – Edward Hopper – 1942

Contents

1 – Ice Change

2 – Last Words

1 – Ice Change

Ice Change

When the Antarctic Winter set in
with its 6 months of perpetual dark
apart from the ghostly light of stars

planets   moon   on snow

And there was nothing to see
and nowhere to go
he began to sink/think/sink

descend   into his own head

And the language he had
had relied on all these years   froze
couldn't begin to measure

never mind express what he was feeling

And as he searched to find the words
his face suffered an ice change
gave up its craggy stress

became smooth   bland

And his voice softened to the whisper
of the rasp of nylon gloves
grasping a synthetic rope

as heard through an anorak hood

In the gap

between work and leisure
a list of things to do

But first   I'll take five minutes
with our local paper
check the obituaries
look at Cluff's cartoon
see what's on the telly
kick off my shoes
change into comfortable trousers

savour my Denby mug   big with tea

Think
It's good to have her home
out of the blue
Only last week said to Barbara
how she'd never caused me any trouble

She rounds us up
and takes us to her room
the room I've just re-decorated
adult cool blues and stripped floorboards
I sit in the newly painted rocking chair
her Dad sits on the bed settee

Do you need us both
Is it something that will keep

After *yes* and *no*   she hands us both a letter
I read mine   rock a little   cannot speak for half an hour

Sound Bite
(10.9.99)

low level whoosh/zoom   constant cars
click   hit   ill-fitting manhole cover
grind/clatter/clank   empty truck

two birds compete   *chip chip chip*
other giggles *he he he*
tock tock tock of the ice cream clock

that Frances made in DT   bubble
and steam of Teasmade   rattle
of door handle brings almost silent tread

of returning dawn-worker   chinks
of cups as he pours the tea and hands
it over to me in bed   My pen writes

no sound that I can hear   tympani
and skiffle as I scratch my head   NO WORD
between us as he shuts the door

that it was thirty years ago today
when first we kissed   stayed up all night
deaf, dumb and blind to anything

but the passion

Recipe

Take one broken heart
beat it to buggery in a glass bowl

Blend, in a separate dish
sweetness of revenge and undigested bile

Whisk both together
Leave to curdle into a sour dough. Later

fold in a pinch, fruits of deceit and, for gravitas
add some dates you'd rather not remember

Pour in a few drops of tears to season
Knead until you've lost all reason

Mould the sticky mixture into a closed shell
Bake, until rock hard, on a high heat

Place on a wire tray until quite cool
Wrap in impermeable greaseproof

Store in a sealed tin on the top shelf
Permit no moisture to seep in

Chill well before serving

On Listening to 'Left Field'

Wail high and thin enough to pierce my skin,
the skin I've grown over the scar,
the scar that is stronger than the skin,
the scab that covers up the wound
that hides all feelings, keeps them in.
The scab that stops me feeling anything
except the muzzy touch of low-level existing.

Just keep it bandaged up so nothing, nothing,
nothing, nothing, nothing, nothing, nothing,
nothing, nothing, nothing, nothing,
nothing can get out or in   again.

Out to Dry

She cannot face the morning unless she's done a line.
A habit she's no desire to kick. Weather is immaterial.

Clothes in a jumbled mess, she checks the paraphernalia.
Follows the daily ritual. Procrastinates. Anticipates.

She's ready to go. Measures out the fine white powder, sniffs,
Clicks, sets cycle with spin. Breakfasts, showers, styles her hair.

Enough time left, and enough rope for a single hanging,
She pegs out.

My Head in a Closet

after a three-dimensional mixed media work by Mary Cozens-Walker

I've put my head in this small cabinet,
embroidered over most of the glass front.

I've left him a small square clear window so
he can catch a glimpse of me, if he wants.

If he slips the catch and opens the door,
he can see a lot more, but only my

head and only the exterior. I'm
not letting him come any nearer. He'll

have to imagine my neck, torso, breasts,
arms, thighs, legs, thoughts.

Studio – living with the artist

after a painting by Kandinsky, Complex-Simple, 1939

You've hung your bag up, but I don't know why
How can you hang it from a thin air hook?
It doesn't make much sense with all this mess

Are those your legs above the crescent moon
dance-bandying from enormous brick red drawers
inverted in a square of bright blue sky

your upper body missing, while your head
is trapped between two multicoloured snakes
and one is spitting bile?   I hate your mess

your mottled mix of harsh and rounded shapes
Formica-souled and careless of my needs
why don't you paint the fucking walls instead?

Pick up your palettes and banana skins
Your dinner's on the table getting cold
I'll try to close the door on all this mess

Waiting Room

– and the trail from specialist department

to specialist department: Breast cancer clinic,
radiotherapy appointment, chest x-ray, mammogram.

And the patients being wheeled through
on their beds, in nighties and drips.

And the shell-shocked pair still functioning
on the receipt of bad news – or only just.

And the man in the basket-weave sandals
in the x-ray queue, rubbing his crutches

up and down his crotch, as though we wouldn't notice
And even though we did, no-one said anything.

And we're not on the trail alone. We're blazing it
for others to stalk in our wake:

from jolly, brave, resigned, naked fear,
– all emotions are on show in here;

to those who've given up, not even
designer scruff, simply sleepy-eyed rough,

and those with varnished toe-nails, immaculate clothes,
faces painted to inane laughter and superficial chatter.

And it's not supposed to be like this, flicking
through magazines we don't see. Shutting out,

pretending we're not really here. How can we be?
We work hard, keep the Law.

Bring our children up to be decent,   kind.
Have our savings in a Pension Plan.

Shadows

From time to time now, she lays out these items,
always the same objects, always the same order.

She takes from the sideboard the white damask linen –
the sort you find in Charity Shops – roses,
harebells, leaves, woven into the background.

She unfolds it, feels sharp starched creases,
spots the faded indigo stain where Tom blotted
his pen doing his Latin homework,

smoothes it against her powdered cheek,
lays it over the dining table.
She places to the right of the central ironed fold:

a willow pattern plate, and matching tea cup
(no saucer), a serviette, same as the cloth,
freed from its horn serviette ring;

on the left, a small jam pot with silver spoon
and lid crowned with a bunch of china cherries.
There is no hint of food, no tea in the cup,

only shadows cast, which are ephemeral,
only the ghosts of tea parties – the cloth
laden with crockery, cutlery, cakes,

sandwiches, orange squash in glasses,
milk in a jug covered with beaded muslin.
And noise. Mother pouring tea, laughing,

Father, smacking his lips round thick jammy
scones, children picking the wings off fairy buns
to lick out the butter icing.

Soon, they will stay in the cupboards
and drawers, wait for house clearance.

Sox

After what seemed like years
of plucking up courage
she wrote her Mum a note
and left it when she went to school,

I want to be the same as all the rest.
At sickening home-time
her Mother said, *I got your note.*
She gave up hope.

On Saturday without a word
her mother took her to the town
bought her a white suspender belt
pink ribbon threaded through,

and stockings.
It seemed a shallow victory
and nothing was resolved except
she knew she'd never feel such pain again.

Bike

They didn't have a car. Her father
took her to the Auction Sale
when she was eight. He bought

an adult's bike for two pound ten
sit-up-and-beg, with basket
on the front, and miles too big.

She couldn't even sit on it
and reach the ground. It had to do
while all the others had brand new.

Dream

Enter
the lift.
It looks tatty.
You ignore your instinct
to wait for a better
one. You've queued for long enough.

As soon as the doors rattle shut
you regret your mistake. But it's too late.
You're whisked up with unsuitable company. The lift tilts,
takes you over the top. Past point of no return.

Rutland Water

in that afternoon the revelations weren't only of the promises of flesh, but of resignation – (*Still Life*, CK Williams)

although I've only just realised this, caught up at the time in beauty,
heat, a glint in the eye and on the man-made lake, oblivious to any
        detail,
aware of a hint of passers-by who might be showing an interest in
        long legs twined
and battleship grey eyes sinking in the deep brown pools of the gaze
        of the other,
as the tiny reservoir and the July day seemed to stretch
        forever,   so loaded
that I could beat into a dark corner any fleeting reservations,
as though time would set its watch to our snatched timetable
and we knew it would happen and that it would be perfect, too
        perfect
if that were possible.   And that it would come to an end.

Abandoned

After the title of Naomi Dum Blake's sculpture in the garden at Beth Shalom Holocaust Memorial Centre. She has dedicated it to the Dum family's ten grandchildren, who perished in Auschwitz.

It's important that there is a record
in the heart of the English countryside.
'Out of the depths have I called thee, Oh Lord'
'Why do you forget us? Where do you hide?'

In the heart of the English countryside,
Beth Shalom – I assumed was run by Jews;
Why do you forget us? Where do you hide?
In undertakers' suits and uncleaned shoes?

At Beth Shalom, which I assumed was run by Jews,
two Christian brothers, trying to make amends,
in undertakers' suits and uncleaned shoes.
For those who never returned – families and friends,

two Christian brothers trying to make amends.
Formal rose gardens, in memory
of those who never returned – families and friends,
honour 'their courage and their dignity'.

Grandchildren's garden. In memory,
Naomi Blake, sculptress, moulds sadness and rage,
honours 'their courage and their dignity'.
For each, a red rose, a plaque with name and age.

Naomi Blake, sculptress, moulds sadness and rage
for millions who died, those dying now,
for each a red rose, a plaque with name and age.
From Rwanda, Auschwitz-Birkenau,

for millions who died, those dying now
it's important that there is a record.
From Rwanda, Auschwitz-Birkenau,
'Out of the depths have I called thee, Oh Lord'.

Rain

(i) Drought

tornado grey
her car, the colour of the sea
between Southampton and Cowes
whirled through cloudbursts
of insects   collective yellow splat
to glue-patch windscreen

her tongue
was parched
by constant drip
in a drenched desert
where everything was green
except hope

day upon day
dirtstorms of hail
scorched her eyeballs

she longed for a good soaking
of new mown rain and the sound
of dust settling

for the smell of pitter-pattering
for rain   soft and strong

for non-porous
hard unrelenting rain

for sandpaper rain to build
a house upon the rock
to shape it at the speed
a stalagmite grows

(ii) Cloudburst

under the awning
sky turns purple
snake tongue flash
champagne and brown ale
                                        crash

stair rods flay the plastic roof
like bad news
            thing on thing

fever   an ocean empties
vomits its vastness
until there's nothing left to come

morning after   wet breath
mildewsniff

and through it all
steam bellows

(iii) Drizzle

dry and grey under the quiet umbrella
soft as breath is fisherman's drench
playing the river surface like a fly
tempting the trout out
keeping the walkers in
                                        time to think

Le Langage des Mégalithes

A few try to make sense of us,
strain to hear our whispers.
Others inflict their own interpretations,
bend our truth to fit their theories.
Most ignore us or reduce us
to a pile of rocks, a few boulders,
          fluent in many languages.

Each stone a leaf, a page of a journal
unread, we have been standing here
for centuries. Some of our number
have fallen on stony ground,
by the wayside, been choked,
carted away for other purposes,
          remain as we were planted.

Some of us are carved,
line chambered cairns, serve
as a channel for equinox light,
sunrise – midsummer/midwinter.
Landscapes have changed,
locus of interests refocused,
          hang on, bearing silent witness.

Those in power encircle us, fence us,
keep us at a distance, replace us
with a visitor attraction, translate
our messages into something quaint,
incomprehensible. We may as well
be speaking French in England,
          speaking to a people who cannot hear,
          writing for the illiterate.

Slack Wife Gill

Langthwaite   stone has aged well
Leadmine landscape poisoned
and choked
has been cleaned up
only a memory of chimneys
lead-filled plumes of smoke
and ghost
of water's gush   taking the ore
down to sorters and smelters

Gravel paths
barely-covered spoil
bleached grass   bracken
heather springy underfoot
Tourist attraction

In spare March
the sky has a blue
that is as cold as heaven
A few angels of clouds
harp it up above
accompany laughing grouse
and xylophone piping
of clean stream and ice wind

Tucked in a tiny crack
between *Fremington Edge*
and *Booze*   lovely
Slack Wife Gill

Who was she?
What did she do?

Did she meet him here
her illicit lover
before she was hushed
out of *Arkengarthdale*
in disgrace?

And her cuckolded husband
did he still love her?
Did he want her to stay
when the valley   awash
with Methodist Chapel Gossip
rushed her away?

Did he climb
the limestone steps of the beck
up the scar onto the fell?
Were these her initials
REK   he carved on this boulder
when he got halfway

before he followed the poisonous flue
breathed in its fumes?

Thornton Street, Darlington – 1964

From Southend girl
to North East lass

My first summer
in dirty heat

Reflecting greenless
streets seduced me

into Gladstone Street
Baths – once.

Half-doored
poolside cubicles

And the loutish loud lads
peering over the top

at the hard buds
of my emergent breasts

Chest measured
in secret in the bath

at home with a flannel
was it a bust yet?

Same lads in the water
leaping, shouting, swearing

ducking   frightening me
I wasn't used to this.

I liked the sea.

Landlocked

I’m reading a bit from the *Times*
about a solitary Irish Moiled cow,
called Harmony

(who ran amok for 5 miles around the fields
above Barton-on-Sea, jumped off a 70 foot cliff,
and spent the night on the sands, before being winched
to safety by non-striking firemen).

Poor cow,
returned to confinement,
inland, as I was 15 years ago

(ferried by ambulance, in the middle
of the night, from Saltburn-by-the-Sea,
to Parkside Maternity Hospital, Middlesbrough,
the last week before they closed it down).

Porthmeor Beach, St Ives

Beach-combing along the low tide line in the shadow of the Tate
on a lovely late May morning

among the mussel shells and rope and nets
and other bits of jetsam and flotsam things

I came upon the upside down white-with-blue-stripes trainer.
It felt male (I think it was the right), about size 10.

It was Tom who spotted the tail in the heel.
He was going to leave it, but I pulled it out.

I'm not sure what kind of fish it was –
herring, mackerel, sea bream – I'm not good at Nature.

It was silver with a bright pink eye,
the eye of the not long dead.

It looked at me, bade me beware
swimming deep, fatal attraction, perfect fit,   tides.

Pull

In front of the mirror in her parents' bedroom
there is a conch shell. From time to time she'll
creep in and pick it up, look at herself
holding it against her right ear. Her father
tells her it comes from the South Seas.
And she thinks of Bournemouth beach
and their last Summer's holiday. He whispers
Hold it to your ear and you'll hear the waves.

And she can – the sucking pull of the tides
against wooden groynes, the slap of the water.
If you close your eyes, he says, *you can imagine*
the life of the creature who once lived inside
on the sea bed. And she does – it slithers out
to play with sea bass, trapped in deep pools.
She saw her father stand here once, the shell
clamped to his stone-deaf head, a back-to-front

smile, lapping the edges of his greying hair.

Sleeping Fisherman, Ploare 1930
after the painting by Christopher Wood

Behind him, the sky
looks stormy,
white spray kisses the rocks.
A maroon-sailed ketch
lists seaward in the wind
beyond the headland.

He dreams
on the reducing shore,
naked to his waist,
his bare feet lapped
by waves.

He is sound –
shrouded in net,
mackerel in a wicker basket
crooked in the space
between his arm and thigh.

There is a settlement,
a spired church,
a few whitewashed cottages,
some planted trees, a wall,   steps,

the possibility of nightmares,
the inevitable tide.

Light-fingered

At night he comes,
imposes himself, says
'Look at me', creeps
in hospital wards, hums

in hotel corridors, stares
red at you from black TVs,
from digital clocks, whines
through bedroom curtain gap

from neon streets;
he shouts down stars,
muffles dark, threatens
to steal you away to

eternal light, singing
There's no night there,
There's no night there.

Sunday School Prizes

"Be thou an Example"

dreaded the religious ones:
anthologies of Bible stories,
Children's Life of Jesus –
"Improving Reading"
for the Officers' daughter.

Peggy and Joan rescued
me. So did *The Beano*
and *The Dandy* – Desperate
Dan, Lord Snooty and his Pals.
When Granny died in 1958

they left me with Mrs Betton
and Donald, ("You must remember
Donald?") near to Agnes Road Juniors,
so I could go to school. It was a deeply
snowy winter. Howard was billeted

miles away and was allowed
'a little holiday'. Officers' kids
farmed out when parents
went to Councils. And would
the billet have a bedside light,

and would I be allowed to have it on
and read? Or would I have to lie
awake, and watch the intermittent
headlights search the bedroom
ceiling, hour on hour?

Five Find-Outers and a Dog. I remember
Fatty – and adventure.

Intercourse

At thy feet I bow adoring, bending lower, lower still...

In intercourse at hearth and board with my beloved ones.

We used to talk a lot, when I thought of you as He, Father,
Lord, maybe as Lover (never as friend or brother).
Now, I'm stuck in this habit of not speaking.

I think I'll call you *God*, for want of something better.
And I'll let you keep the capital for old time's sake.
I could say, How've you been for this past 30 years

or more? Have you aged? Have you suffered any aches
and pains? Have you been trying to talk to me?
Maybe you didn't know I'm going deafer

by the day, so if you've been whispering
in my right ear, you've been wasting your breath.
(*Breathe on me breath of God*, it always made me laugh.)

You never let me know that even 'holy' men,
may not be trusted. Take that randy bandsman,
who offered me a lift, parked on some waste ground,

slipped his hand up my uniform skirt to find the gap
at the top of my black seamed stockings,
and although I kept my knees firmly together,

managed to feel his way into the leg of my knickers,
before I wrestled with the door handle and burst out
of his car (I think it was a black Ford Cortina).

Perhaps you might apologise for keeping quiet.

Epigraphs from 'The Song Book of the Salvation Army'

Bury my bones

said Cuthbert, *on Lindisfarne*
            a fitting spot   remote   spare
            celtic spirit in the very air
somewhere to stay after all
my bishoply perambulations

But no

a whiff of Viking raids   and his acolytes
took fright, dug up his uncorrupted flesh
trekked him for centuries across the Northeast
and after a long stretch in Chester-le-Street
they set him down in Durham. At last   rest

A light man   his Norman shrine
weighs heavy on his chest

So, what about me?

Take my north-aged bones to lie
by the sea-side warm south of my 50s'
childhood holidays. Put them in a beach hut

On second thoughts, spread them
on the weather-bleached veranda
let them heat and cool, heat and cool
with each rising and setting sun

while behind the half-paned doors, hung
with faded 70s' curtains   there'll be:
two striped canvas deck-chairs
a folding green baize card table

and all the necessary accoutrements
to make a nice cup of tea

Private View
(Dining Room Window)

the bottom of a green wine bottle
an elephant's foot, a fossil
skull of curlew, various rocks
and crystals, curved horn of
Swaledale ram, half-a-dozen
tin-glazed brown storage jars
daffodils in a pot

a high farm with bare trees
the odd moving sheep, two cyclists
on the top road, a red pillar box,
drystone-walled fields, grey sky
black and white peewit rises and dives
rises and dives

Ice week

(i) Walk to Aysgarth Falls

Sunlight glinted on silage
sacks as we walked the railway track

no lines, 2 sheds of corrugated tin
and sleepers, a bright blue gate,

thermal glove on wooden fence.
3 white plastic bags like swans

on the river, reminding me
of *American Beauty.* Falls, mill,

church on the hill, tea and cake
in the Visitors' Centre.

Home,   through ice-deep-rutted puddles
like contours on a map

to big orange moon over Gayle.

(ii) Above Sedbusk
(walking on top of the world)

Pockets of snow
in craters. Dark side

of the moonscape. Sheep shelter
in shakeholes, hunker down

too cold to baa. Crunch of boot
on iced puddles. I can write

my family life in walks.

Monsters buried deep   only
their straw-bleached hair blows

free in this stiff breeze.
Flask tea cools from boiling

to freezing in 30 seconds.
Sod Hole Gill becomes

Shiver Gill

2 – Last Words

The night before I died, when I'd decided I was going,
I rallied, said, "Night, night, Love" to each of them.

Dreamwish

I'm there
so is Mum, but she's straight-backed
no walking frame   no fear

we're Steve-Appleby-thin
our hair is streaming in the wind
stick arms held wide and up
and out in front   with open palms
in celebration   running as though
through soft sand   towards
our never-approaching destination

I'm shouting

Mum, look at me   I'm coming too
and she turns   and smiles

we seem to run for miles
and miles but we cannot get there
and then we do   the building is huge
it was a palace in a previous life   with rooms big enough
to swallow terraced streets   and nothing
in them   except a few effete whispering
groups   the almost silence   like the hush
of admiration in the presence of a famous apparition

I see the 'Toilet' signs

but even after endless corridors   and asking
for directions   I'm never closer

I hear two engineers outside
in the grassy quadrangle debating
the expense of maintaining public
lavatory systems   I can hear the cisterns
flush   but still I cannot penetrate an entrance

and even when at last I stumble
on a strangely sited cubicle
the door won’t shut   I have an audience
and I can’t go   yet in some paradoxical
way   this is a great relief   especially
when I wake up to find I haven’t
wet the bed

D(r)ead

I'm not sure,   but a sick weight
drops like thin rain
which, by the time we get to Leamington Spa

has become drizzle.
Familiar train journey, comfort of the rut
until we get past Birmingham

and my landscape is peopled by the dead.
Coventry, Auntie May and Uncle Fred
lived here in brand new 1960.

The man in the seat opposite
is wearing Oakman trousers.
He sips Virgin tea.

Oxford, last time I was here
I came for Auntie Olive's funeral.
My godmother, she delivered me.

Spinster until 80
she wed the widower
who jilted her 50 years before

had 2 happy years with Bill
in his sheltered bungalow
in Abingdon.

Reading – Tom looks up from his *Artemis Fowl*
complains about some mobile's *Mission Impossible*
ringing tone,   and a squalling brat.

All I hear is what I'm going to: slurred speech
reportage of an arm not working
a signature unrecognisable.

The guard shouts,
Mind the gap.

Order of Service

Mrs Brigadier Elizabeth Crowhurst – (née Hutchins)
entered the International Training College from
Portswood *(nothing about her early life of missed school*
domestic drudgery, then five years of hard labour
in Pirelli's tyre factory to scrape enough money together),

was commissioned as an officer in 1935, and served at
Ottery St. Mary
Crediton
Christchurch
(nothing about her raven hair, her musical laugh,
that she is second-in-command
and has to wash her superior's sanitary rags)

Following her marriage to Captain William Crowhurst
on the 19th May 1937, they served together at
Freshwater
Romsey
High Street, Swansea
Pembroke Dock *(where War breaks out, Frank is born)*
Willesden Green
Bush Hill Park
Ashby
Cottingham
(somewhere in here, her second son is born and
dies an hour later. She has a nervous breakdown)

Gainsborough
Liverpool Bootle *(I am born. They call me Marilyn)*
Wrexham *(Howard is born – a bit of a surprise)*

Keighley *(Frank goes off to University; never really comes back.*
She always said if any of her children had the brains
they'd get the chances she never had)
Barnsley
Wellingborough *(we get the dog)*
Plymouth Exeter Hall

Hadleigh Temple
Darlington Citadel
Ashton-under-Lyne
Derby Central
Ipswich Citadel
(we'd all left home; the dog is put to sleep)
'Aucklands' Missionary Home

They retired from active service on the 1st August 1974
(Dad dies July 75)
We praise God for the years of dedicated ministry, and for her Christian living and witness at Boscombe in retirement.
Born 20 April 1913   Promoted to Glory 11 August 2002

Journey

Darlington, A1
M1, Daventry, Oxford
A34, South-

ampton, Bournemouth to visit
a grave where home used to be

on being called in

white elastic hospital stockings
stopping the blood flow
biting into her soft thighs

it's her stocking toes
I take a look at   peeping out
from under the bed clothes
she was very tall

lying flat on her back
in a hospital nightie
arms tight by her side

she hated that
always slept propped upright
nightmare   trying to find enough
pillows when she came to visit

her arms are still warm
and soft and mottled pink
but her face and neck

have drained   pump
stopped   rictus stare
her poor damp wispy white
overpermed hair

no longer a problem

Lists of Indignities

(i) Flat

After my first fall, social services interfering – all that paraphernalia
so I can stay in my own home.   As well as the usual:
visual bell for The Deaf
some things to make the mattress higher
Bleep alarm medallion
(*I don't wear it)*

New upstairs neighbour poking her nose in
calling the ambulance in the middle of the night when I fell in the kitchen
Carted off to hospital against my will
(*I won't be coming back*)

(ii) Hospital

Young doctor asking if I prefer Lizzie or Elizabeth
  (Well, Mrs Brigadier Crowhurst really, but Mrs Crowhurst will do)
hair in a complete mess
glasses perched above horrid oxygen mask with tube
toothless, in an open-back hospital nightie
hooked up to the drips: glucose, antibiotics
plugged into the catheter
padded for 'double incontinence'
        (let them just get on with it)

Hearing aid – switched off on the bedside table
Nurses shouting at me as though I'm stupid –
not taking enough time and trouble to figure out
how to fit the contraption in my left ear using the *KY* jelly......
which stops it squeaking and wailing
They shout in my stone deaf ear
instead of the one with a glimmer

Talking nonsense before I sink into the coma
        (put the kettle on, I'll kill you)
Losing control
        (let me get up, please, please; I promise I'll be good)
Dying in a 6 bed public ward
        (in front of other people – but not my family)

Death in Hospital

My first thought, *No-one will want her body parts;*
eyes too rheumy to be of use for corneal grafts.

I looked back at Nurse Davy pulling the sheet
over her body, drawing the curtains round her bed.

The other old dears stared out at the trees
round the artificial lake. Doris still singing of past lovers.

Later, I went to reception, collected a paper bag
containing her false teeth and wedding ring of Riesling gold.

Bagging Up (Ward 28)

Size 9 shoes
elastic stockings
all-in-one corsets with suspenders

cotton vest
big knickers
incontinence pads in plastic wrappers

flimsy blouse
pale blue jacket
size 24 tartan skirt, pleated (reconditioned)

false teeth
bifocal glasses
national health hearing aid (replacement batteries)

two never-worn nighties
clean polyester flowery dress, pretty cardigan
for when she went home

and one get-well card
(which she was never well enough to open)

Her Place

In the back of one of her drawers
I found a little silver button hook,
(it must have belonged to her mother)

the sort that Edwardian women used
to button up their boots (or the boots of their mistresses)
which concealed, if long skirts lifted a little in the breeze

that glimpse of the forbidden ankle.

Size

Never marry a woman with big plates of meat
she'll cost you a fortune, Dad told us

sitting next to Mum's size 9s
misshapen by corns and bunions
splayed bigger by her increasing weight

his eyes fixed on the man just getting on the bus
with a neat woman in red size 3s

Porcelain Bird

Why

haven't I
chucked you
in the bin?
Well, you
belonged to
Mum. She

liked you
broke you
kept you
thought you
might be
worth a bob

or two.

Flat

On the kitchen wall, *Elizabeth's pad.*
Fridge magnet, *Elizabeth's place,* stays
because it is.   What's missing?

TV racket, hearing aid whistle, fridge hum,
the fridge puddle (where she slipped,
lay on the floor for three hours

perhaps four, *Bleep Alarm* necklace
in a useless pot near the front door).
That bloody trolley at 5 o' clock in the morning

"I've been in bed since 9 last night,
need it to carry my breakfast in."
Her heavy plod, the swish

of pneumatic cushion as she flops
in her chair "I'm nearly on my knees."
Her voice – loud and very strong,

singing along to *Songs of Praise*
"Get me a drop of water for my pills,
Dear." Her smooth, soft skin.

The sweet scent of *Gay Whisper*.

The Language of Burials

When I first saw her on that hospital bed,
no teeth, pink flowery frock, she said,
"I don't know how I got myself into this hole,
and I don't know how I'm going to get myself out."

Lowering her into the deep cemetery hole, I thought
of the language of burials: selected graves,
reserved graves – what was that term – rotational graves,
and something else. You don't really listen.

And looking at the catalogues of Headstones,
each with a name – *The Webb, The Custer* –
lettering, engraved or raised lead, better
to have the latter if you live a long way away

and you can't come back often to visit
your dead mother.   And you don't want marble,
too porous. It will go green if you're not there
to keep an eye on it, and keep it clean.

I need granite. A hard stone for my hard heart.
Mottled grey of Cornish Granite. She hated grey,
although she talked about a very smart grey costume
after the War.   I wish I'd listened more.

Grave

She asked for a burial
not a cremation,
a last piece of British Territory
for her to be stationed.

She'd saved enough
for funeral costs, a headstone,
a little bit left over for her children
and grandchildren.

We gave her a good send off
at the Citadel: her favourite songs,
that reading from 1 Corinthians 13
on love, comrades in uniform,

SA salute – "Well Done,
thou good and faithful servant". The flag
carried in front of her to the committal
under Silver Birches. A proper

Salvation Army Officer's funeral.

Snapshots

She keeps coming back to me in flashes. Last night it was the
hospital images
the last two weeks before she died when I wasn't there. "I'll tell you
all about it
when you get here," she said. Though, of course, she didn't.

This morning, it's the hole. She didn't like the dark, or cold, or being
shut in.
At her funeral, my two aunties, Edie and Ella, both in their 80s,
laughed

and wiped their eyes, "Lizzie. She was a happy soul. Always looked
after us.
She was our mother." I look at two photographs of her on my
bedroom mantelpiece:

the baby one in a big white frock and incongruous stripy football
socks; the other,
left arm round Auntie Joan (aged 5), 1927, in their back garden.

Mum is thin, dark, tall, smiling her lovely open smile. Fourteen, her
first new frock
(a cheap cotton affair, dropped waist, big checks) falls just below her
knees.

Her shiny stockinged long legs end in black buttoned bar shoes, at
least size 8.
She always liked to smile straight into the camera. *And those letters
I wrote,*
telling her she was OK. Though, of course, she wasn't.

Headstone

‘IT IS I. BE NOT AFRAID’

Goddess shape, the SA crest
sits in the small arc at the top
marks her out as she lies
in the *non-con* section
(near to the Muslims).

Almost a year
and my first visit. I pull
a tiny oak tree from
parched earth, dig soil,
plant lavender, blue grass

and something else
that matches. Water them
well.   We’re on the edge
of drought.   An afterthought
some artificial flowers:

carnation, freesia, rose, anemone,
poppy. I put them in the marble
urn – they’ll fade in time.
The raised lead letters fail to
do her life in 30 words, or less

‘GOODNIGHT, GOD BLESS’

Maybank Road, Plymouth

The woman shall not wear that which pertaineth unto a man, neither shall a man put on a woman's garment: for all that do so are abomination unto the Lord thy God (Deuteronomy 22:5)

Mum's bedroom breathes the doze of *Californian Poppy*
the damp of Izal lingers in the outside lav
kitchen exhales the scent of tinned tomatoes
and cheese on toast

flap of washing stretches across the silence
of carless, cobbled, rubbish-free back lane
and Mrs Pentecost is shrieking for Diane
I don't remember rain

in secret I'm wearing Marks and Spencer's trousers
conspiracy with Mum in seersucker blue
my first – three quarter length and banned by Dad
as anti-scriptural

our front door opens straight onto the long steep terrace
with Salisbury Road Juniors at the top, scholarship class
the chosen forty, my favourite hymn
(in minor) *God is Love*

Anemones

So hard to say
and worse to spell, not
beautiful and nothing
in the way of smell.

Fat, hairy
sap-filled stems and
spiky green apologies
for leaves, your sepals,

cultivated faded
pinks and blues,
dwarfed by black
plastic central heads.

Never a bouquet
for a bride. Old ladies'
flowers, old-fashioned
obsolete. Mum's favourites.

You speak late Spring
to me, although your once
short season's now prolonged
by Chinese silk; you are

spinning dusty vase-bound
spells in Sheltered Bungalows,
sitting on crotcheted doilies
on the tea-stained teak.

Miss Jewsbury's Shoes

Miss Jewsbury had big
feet, walked like a man
in a tweed skirt. We
didn't have much money

and my Mum had big feet,
size 9, the same size as
Miss Jewsbury. Big shoes
were hard to find and when

you did discover them, they
were expensive. Here's a
good thought my Mum
had for making ends meet,

"Miss Jewsbury's got big
feet, ask her what she does
with her old shoes".   "Yeah, OK
I'll just slip that into the frame,

when she's quizzing me
about the Jarrow Marchers."

What Does the Daughter of Salvation Army Officers Wear to the Torch Bearers circa 1969?

There was a line drawn:-
which shoes could be worn
on which occasions.

I discovered from the
      post-plimsoll-wearing-to-torchbearers(don't ask)-week-long-sulk
that the wearing of unsuitable footwear
would reflect badly on my mother.

Dad called the same shoes *pumps*
which always had us giggling
like the line of the song

in intercourse at hearth and home
and our unnecessary stress
on *icy blast* in *Eternal Father strong to save.*

When we moved to Darlington
from Southend-on-Sea
the laugh was on me;

my southern plimmies
became sandshoes, sannies
(and the Sally Army
Sally Bash).

My Mum and Adolf Hitler

My Mum and Adolf Hitler share a birthday
It's hard to tell the two of them apart
This might explain the person that I am

Miss Feather, in the Infants, lit some candles,
"Concentrate children. *Now*, express your thoughts"
"My Mum and Adolf Hitler share a birthday"

was not the sort of thought she wished to hear
I had to stand outside and miss the Christmas party
This might explain the person that I am

At ten, I was court-martialled by the Brownies
for doing the goose step in the Church Parade
"My Mum and Adolf Hitler share a birthday"

was no excuse, apparently.   I learned
it's sometimes best to keep your mouth shut
This might explain the person that I am

Dad fought a lifelong battle with the Devil
My Grandad hero-worshipped Genghis Khan
My Mum and Adolf Hitler share a birthday
This might explain the person that I am

Engine House (Burnt Houses)

Eyes dim, slates gone and losing hair
Once proud, now figure of disgust
She should be taken into care

She's old. She's suffered wear and tear
We know she wouldn't want a fuss
Eyes dim, slates gone and losing hair

We've always tried to do what's fair
Of course we love her   but it's just
she should be taken into care

She cannot manage step or stair
Lost balance   how can we trust
dim eyes, loose slates and loss of hair?

She's frozen, given to despair
She'll soon be ruin, rubble, dust
She should be taken into care

I fear she's gone beyond repair
Dried up, her engine's turned to rust
Eyes dim, slates gone and losing hair
She should be taken into care

Above and beyond

the rule of Durham Cathedral (Benedictine Line
roped-off Saint and Chapel of the Nine Altars

everything closed including the view)
to the back of beyond. We climbed concrete steps

through the woods from swollen Tees to High Force Hotel
me singing in full flood, *Climbing up the golden stairs to glory*

in honour of my newly dead Mum.
Sharp shower in the car park saw us briefly anoraked

but by the time we got to Dirt Pit and the old drovers' road
high beeches – copper, bronze, gold – crowned bright blue sky.

On the tops, we reminisced 'boot on grit', barricaded rights of way
how to find a route through. I've learned this thing about rules

and those who enforce them – it's true
they are both there to be broken.

No arguing with nature though. October sun and our path
start their descent bringing us back down to earth

the call of duty.

Beyond Clichés
on Saltburn Beach

a lonely sandwich and the black dog
and my dead Mum hanging round a lot

and the Saturday surfers   wet suit legs
torsos as hard and young as new winter weather

imagine this weather, the worst weather
for a picnic on the dunes

it was the kind of light that drained all colour
scenery grubby and nothing vivid

except my black dog mood
high tides had washed a lot of sand away

cliffs had slid   turf bunched up at the foot
like the scalded skin of Howard's arm that slipped

down the bone to gather around his wrist
in a soggy bracelet   sea, rough and grey

I had my eyes cast down, studying the shore
then I looked up   it was over the sea

a complete bow   all the colours and more
light so bright it silvered the breakers

inside the bow, sky like old varnish on an old master
outside the bow, the sky was darker

it was like a Gateway to a Golden World
the pier   wet black   a path through

anglers kept fishing, surfers surfed faster
gamblers in the amusements played on

as the light moved   Huntcliff's fields
were painted gold and the murky buildings

caravans, trees   of the seafront town
stood black against its ethereal glow

in all that wet, I was dry and warm
and the ocean rushed and roared with laughter

Southbourne Beach – A Year On

Early morning,   I'm raked clean,
flattened and smoothed by the dream machine.

Another day's rumpling begins; someone paddles
as the sea washes in, washes out, washes in, washes out,

makes space for noisy games, for ranks of deckchairs
windbreaks, parasols and salty towels.

Crumbs from packed lunches tickle me
and I'm scalded by gallons of spilt flask tea.

At dusk, my visitors slope off to board and bed
and leave their imprints sleeping with my dead.

'Domestic Goddess' – forgiveness

Mum was a fan of packet sponges.
'Green's Victoria Sandwich Mix' – her favourite.
I used them to make cakes.

If I made one for a 'Sale of Work',
she told me not to mention it. "A lot of people
don't like dirty-fingered children fiddling with food."

More than once, when someone praised
one of my creations, she took the accolade.
(I'll forgive her.)   She knew

a hard childhood as eldest daughter,
3 older brothers, 4 younger sisters,
the drudgery of family skivvy.

Her Mother, worn out from child-bearing,
took to her bed once a month with a hot water bottle
and a length of rubber piping.

Sent my Mum to darn socks at the 'rec'
while the rest were sliding down the river bank
on tin trays, or swimming in the filthy Itchen.

When she went home with her cobbled efforts
her mother ripped out all the stitching, made her start again.
Mum never was a fan of sewing, ironing, mending.

I learned to sew and iron as a defence. I liked it.
Neat and tidy, precise (not messy like the kitchen).

Advent

Today I clean out the grate, screw
newspaper, lay sticks. The brass,
dingy and dull – poker (plus stand), fender
with dented balls, Victorian kettle & trivet.
And I think of Mum. When she was fit
she'd clean it when she came to visit.

Then, latterly, she'd nag at me to do it.
So, in honour of her annual descent
I'd open up the *Duraglit*
don pink rubber gloves, buff
to high shine and firelight glint,
polish away a year's grime.

Give me a week, and I'll repeat the ritual.
No less urgent now she's not here to see it.

Glory

'What are these which are arrayed in white robes? and whence came they?' (Revelation 7:13)

So what is this glory then, that I've been promoted to?
Will the promises come true? *Deep and wide, deep and*
wide, There's a river flowing deep and wide. Crossing the
Jordan? Going over to the other side? A place prepared?
A house with many mansions? Will I meet up with Mum
and Dad, Frank, Trixie, John, Jim? (not all of them Believers)

And Will – will he be 66 or might he, born again, have hair,
have lost his furrowed brow? Will I know him? Will he wear
white, have wings? Will he start telling me what to do?
Will I be able to talk or will there be silence (for as long as half
an hour)? I won't like that. Will there be gadgets, telly, comfortable
chairs? Will there be washing, ironing, cleaning, cooking, eating?

And Paul, my hour-old son, will he be a baby still, try to suckle
at my empty breast? Or will my breasts be full again? Will I be
89? Might he speak, call me Mum? Will I be able to hear? Will
all the arthritis pain drain away? And will there be *No night there*?
Do we sleep, or are we awake 24/7 (as they now say)? Will there
be *no parting there*? Will it be home? Will it be heaven?

Sitting Among the Hoppers

for Mum after a painting of her on Bournemouth beach

Sitting among the Edward Hoppers she is out of place,
a large deck-chaired woman in a print dress,

stuck here after years of travelling,
terminus reached, framed on my landing.

She holds a flask lid – a cup of tea,
stares from under her straw hat straight out to sea:

her young self cycling round Dorset,
Salvation Army Self-Denial collecting,

and, if opportunity arose, 'a spot of courting'.
The Hoppers are brooding:

a sense of unstated menace, their colours –
fox red, pea green, burnt orange, blue marine,

clapboard white – eat the light. Misery seeps
from blinds in bleak American bars, from underneath

shallow brimmed hats.   It blows
in the flimsy frock of the straight-faced gal.

You never wanted to move again,
but now I can't leave you alone

trapped in that sleazy East Coast wasteland.
Stop bothering me.   I know

you never felt comfortable in licensed
premises, unless it was to sell the *War Cry*.

Beforeword – Did I Mention

that she was beautiful

that men stopped in the street
when she walked by

that she was shy
romantic, doomed to disappointment

that she was good
at drama, adored children

that she was tall, slender
had perfect teeth, eyesight, hearing

that she was full of fun
had a great sense of humour

that she was all of these things
before I knew her?